© 2021 by Anniece Ericka Luddy

1st Edition

All rights reserved. No part of this publication may be reproduced, distributed or transmitted in any form or by any means, including photocopying, recording, or other electronic or mechanical methods, without the prior written permission of the publisher, except in the case of brief quotations embodied in critical reviews and certain other noncommercial uses permitted by copyright law.

ISBN: 978-0-578-39662-0

For my beautiful niece, Chasidy.
I know your dad is smiling down on you.
May you read this and always feel inspired. I love you.

A triangle is a universal symbol that dates back to the earliest years of civilization. It can be used to embody varying interpretations depending on religion, spirituality, or orientation. Spiritually, it can represent the different stages of progression and ascension to an omnipresent being. A triangle can also be used to represent manifestation, enlightenment, and creativity, just to name a few.

1
Celebrate you, always.

2

**Commit
to your vision
and be the CEO of your
life.**

3
What you want to be tomorrow, you've got to do today.

4
You are what you allow yourself to become.

5

Work on your strengths.

6

It's never too late to begin again.

7
You dont need permission to be great.

8
Leaders make a way.

9

**Be comfortable with
the unknown.**

10
Manifest your dreams by speaking life into them and envisioning them.

11
Becoming successful doesn't begin with action but belief.

12
What others think of you is none of your business.

13
Never settle.

14
It's the courage to continue that counts.

15
**Life is not just a process
of discovery but
a process of creation.**

16

Be gentle with yourself.

17
Get up, dust your shoulders off and go harder.

18
**Affirm to yourself:
I can and I will.**

19
Accept yourself while your changing.

20
But first, you.

21
Once you put your mind to something, it is already yours.

22
You are living your ancestors wildest dreams.

23
Your potential is limitless.

24

The best way to start anything, pray.

25
There is a breakthrough with your name on it.

26
Find the good and praise it.

27
God never performs his greatest victories in your past, they are always in your future.

28
Connections are made with the heart not the tongue.

29
You have something the world needs.

30
Focus on what you can control.

31

For things that may seem impossible, break them down into small manageable tasks.

32
Think before you speak.

33
If you save money you will always have options.

34
Happiness is a choice.

35
Resolve to do something every single day that moves you towards your goals.

36
Write it down and watch it come to life.

37
**Keep going,
you didn't come this far
to only come this far.**

38
Breakdown or breakthrough?

39
Start complimenting.

40
Outwork
the old you.

41
Nobody is going to save you but you.

42
Trust the process.

43

The greatest gift you can give yourself is the gift of love.

44
Elevate.

45
Quit remembering what god has already forgotten.

46
Have faith that everything is working out for you.

47
**Build.Work.Dream.
Create.**

48

If you give them the power to feed you, you also give them the power to starve you.

49

You become like those whom you most closely associate with.

50
Relinquish Control.

www.ingramcontent.com/pod-product-compliance
Lightning Source LLC
Chambersburg PA
CBHW042310150426
43198CB00001B/32